Thaís Da silva Natal

Deaf young people and inclusive music education

Thaís Da silva Natal

Deaf young people and inclusive music education

A guide for educators

ScienciaScripts

Imprint

Any brand names and product names mentioned in this book are subject to trademark, brand or patent protection and are trademarks or registered trademarks of their respective holders. The use of brand names, product names, common names, trade names, product descriptions etc. even without a particular marking in this work is in no way to be construed to mean that such names may be regarded as unrestricted in respect of trademark and brand protection legislation and could thus be used by anyone.

Cover image: www.ingimage.com

This book is a translation from the original published under ISBN 978-620-2-03224-7.

Publisher:
Sciencia Scripts
is a trademark of
Dodo Books Indian Ocean Ltd. and OmniScriptum S.R.L publishing group

120 High Road, East Finchley, London, N2 9ED, United Kingdom
Str. Armeneasca 28/1, office 1, Chisinau MD-2012, Republic of Moldova, Europe
Printed at: see last page
ISBN: 978-620-7-18235-0

SUMMARY

Thanks

I would first like to thank Professor Dr.[a] Margarete Arroyo for starting this research with me during my scientific initiation. I would also like to thank Professor Dr. Wladimir Mattos for agreeing to continue this research in the final stages of my degree and for his patience. I would also like to thank Professor Dr. Iveta Maria for accepting my invitation to sit on my panel. And I can't forget to thank my parents, who for all these years, since the beginning of my music career, have never abandoned me and have always given me all the support possible and necessary.

Summary

The subject of this research is young deaf secondary school students and their relationship with music. The aim is to understand how deaf young people relate to music and to indicate the implications of this relationship for pedagogical-musical practice. This is a qualitative investigation with data collected through questionnaires and interviews with young people.

According to the interviews, I was able to analyze that the musical styles they like the most are those with an accentuated mark, such as rock, funk and electronic music. It is hoped that the results achieved will help music educators to plan and make the necessary adaptations to inclusive music lessons.

Keywords: Deafness, young people, music, pedagogy.

1. INTRODUCTION

This research is about deaf young people and their relationship with music and is an extension of
the studies carried out in the scientific initiation research entitled Deaf young people and inclusive
music education, under the supervision of Prof. Margarete Arroio, who also signed the Term of
Commitment related to the questionnaire applied as a methodological procedure (as we will see
below).

My interest in this subject arose from my efforts to work in music education for students with
disabilities. In this work, I focus on young people with deafblindness, whether or not they use
hearing aids or cochlear implants. I want to understand how these young people interact with music
in their daily lives, since this form of expression is very present in the lives of most people who live
through this stage of life. I also intend to raise some aspects about how music education could be
worked on in an inclusive classroom, with the presence of students who have normal hearing and
students with deafblindness.

The return of compulsory music at school, in accordance with Law 11.769/2008, as well as the new
educational policies of inclusion, which proposes the inclusion of students with physical disabilities
in regular classes, makes it necessary for teachers to update their pedagogical knowledge and skills.

Decree No. 5.626,2006 states:

Art. 14 (IV) Federal educational institutions must guarantee deaf people access to communication, information and
education in the selection processes, activities and curricula developed at all levels, stages and modalities of education,
from early childhood education to higher education. (BRASIL, 2006)

In the same chapter, § 1 paragraph IV guarantees

Meeting the special educational needs of deaf students, from early childhood education onwards, in classrooms and also
in resource rooms, in the opposite shift to schooling. (BRASIL, 2006)

It is true that deaf young people have significant restrictions compared to young people who have
had the typical development of hearing, other senses, physical and cognitive abilities. However,
this does not exclude the possibility of these young people developing some level of musical ability
and, consequently, some interest in music.

In order to work on music education with deaf young people, as well as young people with normal
hearing, we need to understand their relationship with music and how it affects their daily lives.
Nowadays, access to information is made much easier by digital technologies. We can find videos

of vocal music on the internet with texts translated into LIBRAS and this can be favorable for deaf young people's relationship with music. But in the case of instrumental music, how would this relationship work?

The general objective of this research is to study the relationship between deaf young people and music, in terms of learning music in their daily lives.

The methodological procedures followed a qualitative approach and involved observing young people with deafblindness in public places, as well as structured interviews with them. In the original plan, it was hoped to interact with students from a specific school, but the difficulties of insertion into the institution required a re-planning. Thus, the young people interviewed were contacted in a public place where they spontaneously found themselves, the Santa Cruz subway station in the city of São Paulo. Observations also took place at the XII International Fair of Technology and Rehabilitation, Inclusion and Accessibility (REATECH). Other unforeseen resources were included in the data collection. These were materials available on the internet such as videos, blogs and websites whose content dealt with the relationship between deaf young people and music.

2. OBJECTIVES

2.1 GENERAL OBJECTIVES

> Understanding deaf young people's relationship with music

2.2 SPECIFIC OBJECTIVES

> Understanding deaf young people in terms of learning music in their daily lives.

> Review the literature on deaf people and music learning.

3. RESEARCH METHODOLOGY

The methodological procedures were qualitative in nature. Data was collected by means of questionnaires and interviews aimed at deaf young people on how music plays a part in your life, how you deal with it in your daily life.

The young people were selected on the basis of their voluntary agreement to take part in the research and were contacted in public places in the greater Sao Paulo area, Jabaquara subway station, Santa Cruz subway mall and 12^a International Fair of Technology and Rehabilitation, Inclusion and Accessibility (REATECH).

4.   literature review

This bibliographical review aims to situate the research topic and is organized into the following "sub-themes": deafness, deafness and musical experience and being young and music.

5. THE SOUND

First of all, before talking about deafness, we need to understand the characteristics of sound and how it propagates in space.

Sound comes from the sound wave, which is the vibration of molecules around their equilibrium position or state of rest, causing a disturbance in their state, which can be solid, liquid or gaseous. After the disturbance occurs, the molecules return to their starting point. When a vibration occurs, our ears pick it up and cause our tympanums to vibrate, which starts our perception of sounds.

Hearing is essential in the relationship between living beings and the environment in which they live. Through sound, living beings can defend themselves against possible threats, feed themselves or reproduce. In the case of human beings, hearing plays an important role in the development of oral language so that they can better socialize and communicate in the environment in which they live.

The vibration of sound is coded in the cochlea (inner ear) and transmitted to the brain by the auditory nerve. When this vibration reaches the brain, the neurons decode the message received so that when it reaches the auditory cortex, we can identify the quality of the sound as accurately as possible from the original sound.

Sound in turn has 4 properties:

Height: Height is the property that characterizes sound. This sound can be high-pitched (a thinner sound) or low-pitched (a thicker sound). The quality of the sound in being high-pitched or low-pitched is related to the frequency of the sound wave, the faster it is (the greater the number of vibrations per second) the higher the pitch, the slower it is (the lower the number of vibrations per second) the lower the pitch.

Intensity: Intensity is the property that a sound has of being stronger or weaker than another. For example: A person shouting has a stronger sound intensity than a person whispering, who would have a weaker sound intensity.

Duration: The duration is the time that the sound will propagate through the material without interruption, this duration can be long or short.

Timbre: Timbre is what allows us to know the origin of the sound source, this is done through the quality and characteristic of that sound, it is through timbre that we can identify whether it is a male voice, a female voice, an adult voice, a child's voice, a flute, a piano, a car, a motorcycle... It is through timbre that we can differentiate one sound from another.

As already mentioned, for sound to propagate it needs a material medium, solid, liquid or gaseous. Depending on the medium, sound will propagate faster or slower. In air, sound has an average speed of[1] 340 m.s^{-1} , which means that sound travels 340 meters. In vacuum, however, as there are no particles, sound does not propagate.

Sound is received through the ear. The human ear is capable of detecting sounds with frequencies between 20Hz and 20000Hz. We can find 3 stages of sound frequency:

INFRA -SONS: Sounds with a frequency lower than 20HZ

SOUNDS: Sounds with a frequency between 20Hz and 20000Hz

ULTRA-SONS: Sounds with frequencies above 20000Hz

[1] Reference: https://pt.wikipedia.org/wiki/Som

6. DARKNESS

Deafness is the partial or total loss of hearing caused by genetic dysfunction or injuries and diseases that can be acquired during pregnancy or during / after birth until old age. It can occur in one or both ears.

Hearing loss during childhood can affect language development, causing difficulties in adolescence and work in adulthood. According to the 2010 Census, the following table shows the number of people with some degree of deafness in Brazil[2]

Hearing impaired 9,722,163

Can't hear at all 347,481

Great difficulty 1,799,885

Some difficulty 7,574,797

[3]According to the World Health Organization, every 1,000 births are diagnosed with 1 to 1.5 cases of severe or profound deafness, and this figure rises to 3% if cases of moderate deafness are included and to 5% if all cases of hypoacusis are included.

Three quarters of cases of deafness are genetic (g). The other quarter are acquired during pregnancy or the perinatal period.

Most cases of deafness are due to problems of the middle ear (OM) such as chronic otitis or otitis media with effusion or seromucosa.

The percentage of cases of hypoacusis with a genetic cause is reduced to approximately 10%.

The rest (blue) is caused by multiple factors.

The factors that cause adult deafness are on the increase and now account for the vast majority of deafness cases.

[2] Data taken from: http://sulp-surdosusuariosdalinguaportuguesa.blogspot.com.br/2012/05/censo-do-ibge- 2010-data-about.html

[3] Text taken from: http://www.cochlea.org/po/surdez

Chronic otitis media (OM) only accounts for 20% of cases, less than Menière's disease (M), which also affects the vestibular system (vertigo). Acoustic trauma (t), caused by overexposure to sound, now ranks first among the factors responsible for deafness... and its importance can only increase.

Other factors complete this graph: mainly ototoxic drugs and sudden deafness. Deafness of genetic origin (g) only accounts for a small percentage of the total, but it should be noted that in many cases (acoustic trauma, ototoxicity, Meniere's, etc.) it is likely that there are genetic components that accelerate acquired deafness.

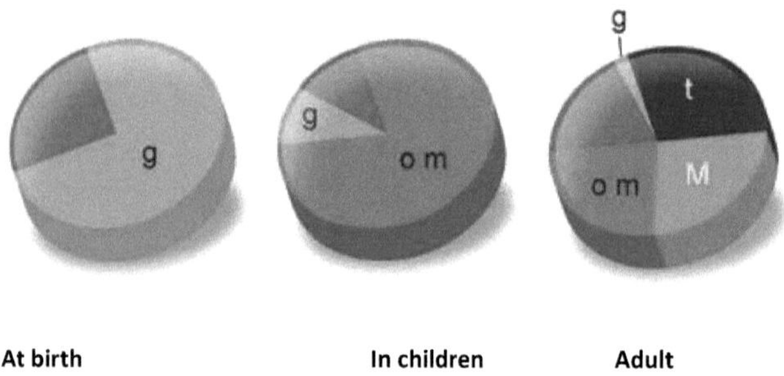

At birth   **In children**   **Adult**

It is through our ears that we can find one of the main means of communication. When we meet a deaf person, their way of communicating changes according to their family environment. We can divide this environment into: deaf children of deaf parents, deaf children of hearing parents, hearing children of deaf parents, hearing children of hearing parents. These different environments interfere with the individual's learning and mother tongue.

The way in which deaf people were seen in the past is very different from how they are seen today. The Greeks saw a deaf person as an animal, because for them, if a deaf person couldn't speak, then they couldn't think. For the Romans, a deaf person had no legal rights, couldn't marry or be heir to the family. For Catholicism, a deaf person would not have divine salvation, that is, they would not reach the kingdom of God. When a child was born deaf, he or she could often be considered to have some kind of intelligence *deficit*, since, as a result of not being able to hear, the child did not typically pay attention to the events around him or her and did not develop speech. Ponce de León, a deaf Benedictine monk, initiated a change in the way deaf people were perceived. Ponce de León dedicated himself to teaching deaf children of noblemen to read, write, speak and learn the doctrines of Catholicism.

After León, other advocates emerged, all of whom believed that speech was essential for the development of a person's intellect, as well as the recognition of deaf people as citizens, which would consequently give them the right to receive family inheritance. In England we find John Wallis, considered the founder of oralism.

In the book Seeing Voices by Oliver Sacks (1998, p. 38) we can find an account of the situation in antiquity where he reveals the fragility of the defenders of oral communication.

"There were, in fact, real dilemmas, as there always were, and they still exist today. What was the point of using signs without speech? This would not restrict the deaf. In everyday life, to relationships with other deaf people? Shouldn't they be taught to speak (and lip-read) instead, allowing them to integrate fully with the general population? Shouldn't sign communication be banned, so as not to interfere with speech?"

Nowadays, we know that being deaf is not necessarily associated with an intelligence *deficit* and that we can treat the different types of hearing impairment from intrauterine age, especially in cases related to malformation of the auditory organ and in neurological cases.

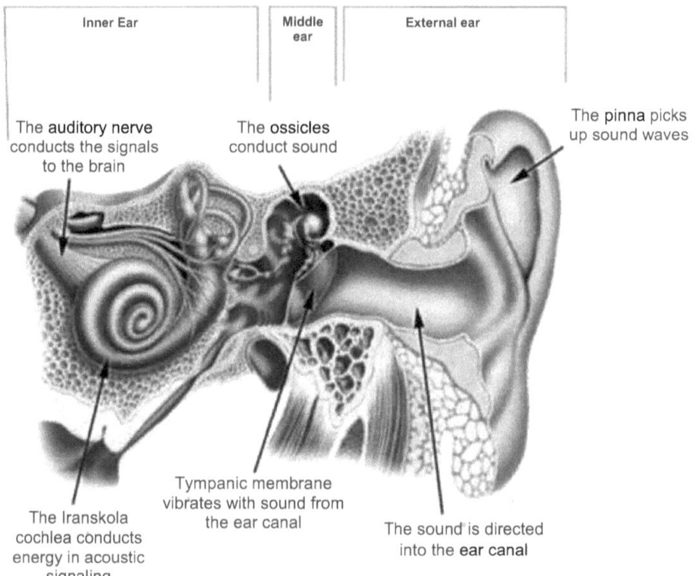

Understanding the characteristics of deafness requires some understanding of the construction of the hearing organ. According to Afonso (2012), the ear is subdivided into three parts: inner, middle and outer.

The organ used by humans to detect sound waves is the *ear* which, under normal conditions, is capable of detecting around 400,000 different sounds in a sound frequency range of approximately 20 to 20,000 Hertz. The ear (officially) or ear (alternatively) is classified into three parts: external, middle and internal.

The ear is made up of the pinna and the ear canal. The main function of the pinna is to collect sounds and direct them into the ear canal.

[...] [The] middle ear, formed by the tympanic membrane, [consists of] three very small bones - named after their resemblance to certain objects (hammer, anvil and stirrup) - and the auditory tube. The sounds, after reaching the tympanic membrane through its vibration, are relayed to the hearing axes, which form a system of levers, exciting the next structure in the system, called the oval window, by means of a solid. [...] The inner ear is essentially made up of the cochlea and the vestibular apparatus, the latter of which plays a role in our balance (AFONSO, 2012, p.170 and 171).

As for hearing loss, we can group it into four different forms: conductive, sensorineural, mixed and central hearing loss. According to Afonso,

Conductive hearing loss is when there is a failure or interference in the transmission of sound from the pinna to the end of the middle ear. [...] Sensorineural hearing loss occurs when there is damage to the inner ear (cochlea) or the auditory nerve. [...] Mixed hearing loss, as its name suggests, is when there is an alteration in the pattern of sound conduction. This alteration is linked to damage to the inner ear or the auditory nerve. [...] Central hearing impairment is not always accompanied by decreased sensitivity to sound stimuli; it refers to decreased sensitivity and interpretation of sound information in the central nervous system. (AFONSO, 2012 p.173)

Factors that can determine hearing loss or conductive hearing loss:

- Anotia (during pregnancy the outer ear is not formed)

- Microtia (probably non-functional outer ear due to lack of growth, small outer ear)

- Atresia of the auditory canal (unformed canal without sound transmission)

- Stenosis of the ear canal (congenital or acquired origin causing narrowing of the canal)

- Onion cysts (formation of lumps under the skin)

- Infections and others.

Sensorineural hearing loss:

- Congenital infections during pregnancy (rubella, syphilis, others)

- Post-natal infections

- Physical trauma

Mixed hearing impairment:

- Genetic syndromes

- Injury to the inner ear or auditory nerve

Central hearing loss:

- Changes in the brainstem up to the subcortical regions and cerebral cortex.

The degree of hearing loss, taking into account that a normal person can perceive sounds between 0 and 24dB, can be found:

- Mild hearing loss: 24 and 40 dB

- Moderate hearing loss: 41 to 70 dB

- Severe hearing loss: 71 and 90 dB

- Profound hearing loss: 90 dB upwards

It's common to think that these people are deaf and mute, but this is due to the impossibility of sound imitation that occurs because of the individual's disability. For this reason, when we hear a deaf person expressing themselves, we often hear some vocal noises, which often frighten listeners who are not used to living with deaf people.

Due to this factor and the lack of knowledge about LIBRAS, one of the main consequences of deafness is the difficulty of communication between deaf and hearing people. This deprivation can cause distrust and insecurity in all participants in the communication process.

According to data found on the Wikipedia website[5] , some of the characteristics of deaf speech would be:

- High-pitched or low-pitched voices with timbre fluctuations;

- Poorly controlled voice intensity;

- Lack of rhythm with extreme difficulty in maintaining the right tempo for each phonetic production;

- Difficulty with breathing and speech;

- Difficulty or absence of accentuation with deformations in melody, temporal and dynamic accent;

- Articulatory difficulties with omission, dropping or substitution of phonemes.

---

[5] http://pt.wikipedia.org/wiki/Surdez

7. YOUTH AND DEAF CULTURE

First of all, we need to know who young people are and how they relate to deaf culture.

I remember my youth, the desire for madness, challenges, wanting to go out into the world with no final destination. The young person is the one who isn't afraid of danger. I once heard about an event that took place once a year in the city of Sao Paulo, where people were given a pair of tickets to plays and musicals that were on. The distribution points for these tickets were scattered around the center of Sao Paulo, such as the Teatro Municipal de Sao Paulo, Centro Cultural Vergueiro and libraries. The first year I took part in the event, I arrived 20 minutes before the start of the distribution, which was scheduled for 2pm. When I arrived, I was faced with a huge queue, and of course the tickets for the Broadway musicals were nowhere near my hands, the average number of tickets was 80 per play. The following year, I made up my mind to be one of the first in line. To do so, I had to arrive very early. I took the first subway at 4:40 in the morning and went to the Anhangabaù Valley to stand in line in front of the Teatro Municipal de São Paulo. I was the first in the queue and 30 minutes after my arrival others joined me. But now I'm thinking, how crazy to be alone at the height of my 20s in the center of Sao Paulo, sitting on the floor fiddling with my cell phone, reading a book at 5 o'clock in the morning. That moment for me wasn't just about winning a pair of tickets, but the adventure itself of being there in the face of danger.

This is the young person who likes to venture out into the world. According to Ozella and Aguiar (2008, apud MADELLI et al, 2011) adolescence is:

[...] understands young people from a denaturalized perspective. Thus, the meanings of adolescence are constructed in the dialectical relationship between objectivity and subjectivity, and there is no natural adolescence. The signifier "adolescence" is not denied, but neither is it understood as a phase of development, or as universal. The scientific interest comes from understanding how adolescence is historically constructed, rather than understanding what it is, in an attempt to create an almost natural identification.

Deaf young people have the same desire for challenges and adventures as hearing young people, but they have even greater challenges - communication. We live in a culture where sign language is neither taught nor valued, and these young people often feel excluded from society as a whole, whether at college or at work.

Sign language and oralism has been a major dilemma in deaf culture since ancient Greece. Aristotle said that those born deaf had no language and therefore could not reason. Seneca said[6]

"We kill dogs when they are angry; we exterminate wild bulls; we cut off the heads of sick sheep so that the rest are not contaminated; we kill fetuses and monstrous newborns; if they are born defective and monstrous, we drown them, not because of hatred, but because of reason, to distinguish useless things from healthy ones."

Socrates, for his part, declared in 360 BC that it was acceptable for the deaf to communicate with their hands and bodies.

Society has always made great efforts to ensure that the deaf can hear and speak (oralized deaf), because as already mentioned, they believe that they can only reason if they learn language. Mabel Gardiner Hubbard became deaf at the age of 5 after a fatal attack of scarlet fever. She was one of the greatest defenders of oralism, saying that a deaf person should not communicate with their hands and could not marry another deaf person, as this would put society at risk. Hellen Keller, who became deaf and blind at the age of 19 months, created more than 60 gestures to communicate with her family.

It was during the 18th century that the terms *Gesturalism* (the French method) and Oralism (the German method) emerged, with the majority of deaf people, especially those born deaf, defending Gesturalism and the majority of hearing people, or those born hearing, defending Oralism. This dispute between the two forms of learning can still be found today, causing a great deal of conflict within the deaf community.

The first hearing aid was created in 1898 where acoustic tubes helped to amplify sound and in 1948 the first hearing aid with built-in batteries appeared. In 1970, the first attempts at cochlear implantation were made, where many hearing parents wanted to use this method when their child was born with deafness, and many of the implanted children rejected the implant. I was able to experience this situation with a student who, for the sake of image confidentiality, I call Daniel, who had problems during pregnancy which caused his deafness. When I started teaching Daniel's class, he didn't have a cochlear implant. The classes with him were very challenging, because for him that environment didn't make sense, he didn't know how to communicate with sign language and he wasn't oralized, he was in an environment where only he was deaf and there was no effort to communicate by gesture. At just over 4 years old, Daniel underwent the cochlear implant procedure. When he arrived at school, he rejected the device, it was a daily fight, because for him the noises and sounds were a nuisance. That's why the deaf community doesn't support cochlear implants for children before they develop language, because you're forcing a deaf child to be hearing.

Young people who have studied in a bilingual special school tend to identify deeply with the deaf community and culture. This is because bilingualism is not restricted to the pedagogical dimension, but must also be seen in its political dimension, as a historical, cultural and social construction, and in the context of relations of power and knowledge (Skliar, 1999). [7]

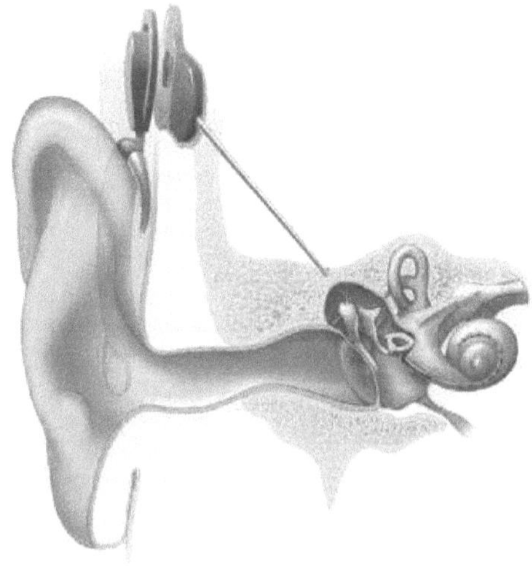

Illustration of the inside of a cochlear implant

Looking at the whole history of deafness and how it is seen today, we can imagine the challenges encountered not only during youth, but throughout the life of a deaf person.

7.1. THE DEAF PERSON AND THEIR MUSICAL EXPERIENCE

However, at first glance, thinking about music and deafness is almost like thinking about mixing water and oil, but these two realities may be closer than you think, despite the fact that there is still relatively little work in the area.

According to Oliver Sacks we can say that

Congenitally deaf people don't experience 'silence' or complain about it

(just as blind people don't experience 'darkness' or complain about it). [...] In addition, those with the most profound deafness can hear noises of various kinds and are sensitive to vibrations of all kinds. [...] The development of the perception of vibrations as an accessory sense has certain analogies with the development of 'facial vision' (which uses the face to receive a kind of sonar information) in the blind (2010, p. 139 - 140).

According to Afonso (2012), deaf people, even if they are profoundly deaf, are able to interact with music. They can hear small noises and feel the vibrations caused by the music, by leaning against

[7] Taken from: http://www.scielo.br/pdf/cp/v40n139/v40n139a08
[8] Image taken from: https://pt.wikipedia.org/wiki/Hist%C3%B3ria_dos_surdos#/media/File:Cochlear_im- plant.jpg

the musical instrument, the speaker or the vibration on the floor.

In crude terms, music is seen as a "rehabilitative crutch". But this is not the case for many deaf people. If given the chance, deaf people not only learn music, they also come to understand its intrinsic importance. Music invites movement, expression and integration. Sound, its raw material, is made up of vibrations. So the deaf - who can't hear their surroundings but can feel the sound vibrations in their bodies - gradually come to understand the musical intentions. Even people with profound deafness can have innate musicality (AFONSO, 2012, p.192).

As we saw above, sound is transmitted through sound waves that propagate through the air and can be perceived by the hearing system. The vibrations caused by this propagation, under certain conditions, can be perceived by other organs in the body, such as the skin and bones. For Haguiata-Cervellini, the artificial resources of sound amplification make it easier for the deaf to perceive sounds, but it is not their only possibility of experiencing sound.

The use of sound amplification devices makes it easier to perceive the world of sound. But it is not only by this means that deaf people can access sound. The vibrations of sound waves can be picked up throughout the body. These can be perceived through the skin and bones. The skin is the most vital sense organ. You can live without hearing, sight, smell and taste, but it's impossible to live without your skin. The skin establishes the boundaries of the body, enabling it to relate to the outside world. It is therefore a fundamental means of communicating with others. It acts as a general transmission channel. It follows that sounds can also affect the subject in this way. And by benefiting from it, the deaf person can also enjoy this world of sound and react to it. Hearing with the body, tuning in to sound vibrations through the whole pericorporeal extension is possible for the deaf, as well as the hearing. The multisensory perceptive set allows them to experience music and thus creates channels for the manifestation of their own musicality. (HAGUIATA-CERVELLINI, 2003, p. 79)

Based on this data, we can talk about the musicality of deaf people. How can they perceive music and how can we see whether or not they have musicality?

Musicality is the possibility that man has of expressing internal music, or getting in tune with external music, through his body and its movements, through his voice, singing, playing, perceiving a musical sound instrument or not, or attentive musical listening. (HAGUIATA-CERVELLINI, 2003, p. 75)

A person can express their musicality by playing a musical instrument, singing a melody they know or created themselves, dancing or even clapping their hands or feet on the floor. So we can't separate music from movement and bodily expression.

The conditions and characteristics of the sound and musical experience of people with deafblindness indicate that they also learn music. What makes this learning different from that of hearing people is the way in which it is carried out. It will often be necessary to adapt teaching materials and methods according to the type of disability in question.

According to Louro; Afonso; Molina (2006, p. 5)

Many believe that music for people with disabilities should only be aimed at rehabilitation. [...] Schools or teachers are often afraid to take any responsibility for the health of a disabled person. However, it is essential to understand that disability is a condition, not a state of health that may or may not be aggravated by an educational practice, whatever it may be.

With these questions in mind, how can we experience music with deaf people? Through my experience in the classroom, I was able to observe Daniel's interaction with music. The classroom didn't have a wooden floor, so all the activities I developed with body movement, circle games and sound stories were rejected by him. However, whenever I introduced a musical instrument or played music by electronic means, he became more involved in the lessons, explored the instruments and held the radio with his hands, so that through the contact between the music and his skin, he was able to find greater meaning in the lesson for him.

Although my experience with deaf students took place in early childhood education, we can think about how to adapt these situations with young people. We saw that the moments of attention were with percussive instruments and electronic music. Young people, like children, need visual and physical contact. As we've seen, low-pitched sounds have the fewest vibrations and are therefore the sound we can most feel and identify in contact with the skin, so the lower the pitch of the instrument, the more interested the deaf individual will be. So if you want to show them the markings, the pulse of a piece of music, you can use visuals with lights, as we'll see below.

7.1. BEING YOUNG AND MUSIC

Another point in question is to understand what relationships the deaf young person establishes with music, given that this artistic language is very present at this stage of life where it is in it that we create our personal playlist, but the deaf young person when putting together his playlist will not only analyze the lyrics or musical style like any other young person, but the one that brings the best sensation to his body, after all for the deaf what attracts him most in a song is in how its vibration relates to his body.

According to Arroyo, "musical practices actively participate in youth constitutions" in today's society (2010, p. 22):

Music is one of the most striking phenomena in youth culture. Studies carried out by British social psychologists have confirmed that "music is of central importance in the lives of most young people, fulfilling social, emotional and cognitive needs" (North; Hargreaves; O'Neill, 2000, p. 269). Aware of the strong presence of music in the daily lives of adolescents and young people, researchers have dedicated themselves to understanding the why and how of this presence (ARROYO, 2007, p. 14).

Understanding the way young people with deafblindness relate to music is important for teachers, as they are responsible for guiding the development of this relationship. Each student, disabled or not, has his or her own difficulty or facility and the teacher has to be prepared to deal with different situations in his or her day-to-day work with regard to the students' conditions. From then on, the teacher must devise strategies to achieve his or her goal of facilitating the student's relationship with music, a goal that must be very clear to him or her before starting any work with a class, be it new or familiar.

As music teachers, we must always remember that many students, regardless of their physical or mental condition, whether disabled or not, will initially approach music lessons as a *hobby* and a few will go on to pursue a career in music.

Some of Haguiata-Cevellini's considerations on adolescents with deafblindness and music deserve attention. The author comments on the comparison of musical skills between deaf and hearing people and issues of deaf people's self-image, based on research she has carried out.

Competing with top musicians, such as Isadora's family, is extremely unfair for a deaf person. The other person's virtuosity and competence end up denouncing the deaf person's "incompetence". So not exposing themselves is a form of self-protection. And in the middle of adolescence, when self-criticism and a sense of ridicule are highly exacerbated, this feeling and the representation of oneself are deeply damaged. The positive self-image that is built up through success and pleasure in achievements becomes unattainable. You then have to rely on other people's approval in order to "feed" yourself. But in this case, it's also difficult to get family approval for the deaf daughter's musical experiences. The level of demand is high and any production is only seen as a small instrument for improving speech, and not as a musical possibility. (HAGUIATA-CERVELLINI, 2003, p. 111)

Haguiata-Vervellini also mentions in her text:

Deaf people are extremely sensitive to criticism and do not respond well to frustration. As a result, they are suspicious of their relationship with the environment, sensitive to failure, disappointment and loss. Their self-image is damaged (HAGUIATA-CERVEL-LINI, 2003, p. 61-62).

In interviews conducted by the author with two deaf girls, we can observe their musicality. One of them is Isadora, a young woman of almost 17. Her father is a professional musician, her mother sings in a choir, one of her brothers is a drummer, the other a bass player. She says she likes music, but music doesn't make a difference to her life.

Isadora took flamenco dance lessons, which indicates her musicality since this style of music requires a lot of rhythmic marking with the body. As well as Flemish music, she likes *rock and roll.*

The other is Fabiana, a 19-year-old who has been taking part in Haguiata-Cervel- lini's research since she was four. Since she was a child, she has shown an interest in music. As a baby, her mother hummed to her and exposed her to music, even when she was diagnosed with deafness. Like her parents, she says she likes calm, slow music, such as sertanejas and pagodes, but she also likes rock. Fabiana loves to dance and sings some tunes.

We can analyze these two young deaf women, both of whom have had direct contact with music since childhood and have shown that they enjoy listening to it. According to Haguiata-Cervel- lini, Isadora's mention during the interview that music makes no difference to her life is a way of demonstrating her inhibition at being part of a family of musicians, and because of her deafness she is unable to compete with her siblings in musical practice.

In our daily lives, we may come across situations similar to these and, as teachers, we should know how to remedy these moments and make these deaf students take an interest in the class and not feel isolated or incapable.

8. MUSICAL LISTENING AND THE RELATIONSHIP BETWEEN MUSIC AND MOVEMENT MENTO.

We know that musical learning is first and foremost related to reception or listening. Listening, in turn, is related to bodily movement. When we listen to music, we naturally move our bodies and by moving, we broaden our relationship with what we hear. That's why we can't stop working with body movement in music lessons, so that it's easier to understand music.

To talk about music and movement, we can mention the music educator Émile Jaques-Dalcroze, who was born in Geneva in 1865 and lived until 1950. He had two main concerns: firstly, the interaction between listening and body movement, and secondly, the mass teaching of music due to the large increase in the population.

According to him, the students intellectually understood the rhythmic organization of the melodies, but were unable to execute them well because they had no control over the movements of their vocal apparatus [...]. Dalcroze's second concern is broader and shows how interested he was in finding solutions to the conditions that were emerging in the new century. Analyzing the issue of music education in his time and country, he gave educational bodies, teachers and artists the responsibility of promoting mass education. (FONTERRADA, 2008, p.123)

Dalcroze sought to unite movement and the auditory experience of sounds, because for him music was made up of sound and movement. From this, Dalcroze created his method called *"Rithmique"*, which emphasizes general education and *"provides instruments for the integral development of the person through music and movement. In addition to this broader purpose, it acts as an educational activity, developing active listening, the singing voice, body movement and the use of space"* (FONTERRADA, 2008, p.131).

Dalcroze believed that in order to work with music you have to turn your body into a big ear, making your body hear the music and not just your ear.

Now what is body expression?

Body expression is a pre-existing spontaneous behavior, both in the ontogenetic and phylogenetic sense; it is a language through which human beings express sensations, emotions, feelings and thoughts with their bodies [...].It encompasses the sensitization and awareness of ourselves, both in terms of our daily postures, attitudes, gestures and actions, and in terms of our need to express-communicate-create-share and interact in the society in which we live (STOKOE, 1987, p.15).).

From this we can then think about how to work with a hearing-impaired person in an inclusive education context. As I said earlier, even the profoundly deaf can hear certain noises, and since music is sound and sound propagates through space by means of a sound wave, we can distinguish a sound with the body by means of the sound's vibration.

Therefore, for the lesson to make sense to the deaf person, the ideal is to hold music lessons in a room with wooden floors, so that when you play a song at a loud volume (through a sound amplifier), you can feel it with your feet (preferably barefoot).

An example of some activities that can be carried out with a class that has both hearing and hearing-impaired students, following the body movement proposal of educator Émile Jaques-Dalcroze:

> FEELING THE SOUNDS

Ask your students to move around the room according to the tempo of the music (fast/slow), remembering that the more you explore the planes (high/medium/low), encouraging them to make basic movements such as walking, running, jumping, crouching, crawling, crawling on the floor, will make the activity work better. If your deaf students, even barefoot and walking on the wooden floor, still have difficulty perceiving the vibration of sound, you could ask them to place their hands on the radio. Another suggestion is to put earplugs on your hearing students, so that even if they can hear a little of the sound, they will be able to perceive the vibration of the sound more easily with their bodies.

> WALKING ON THE WRIST

With the help of a clock, the students watch the movement of the second hand and follow it with steps around the room. The teacher can help the movement by playing a drum with a low sound along with the movement of the hand, then ask each student to feel their heartbeat and move accordingly.

> THE MASTER

This activity is carried out in a circle. One student is chosen to leave the classroom, while another student is chosen to be the master, all the others have to imitate his movement, which can be anything from body movements to different rhythms, clapping hands or tapping feet. The student who was outside the classroom will be called and will stand in the center of the circle and will have to find out who the master student is.

> STATUTE

In the same way as the *feeling the sounds* activity, the students will listen to a piece of music and have to walk around the room according to its rhythm (if the deaf students have difficulty distinguishing the sounds, the teacher can play the pulse with a bass drum). When the music stops, the students should stand still and only move again when the music starts again.

> PASSING THE PULSE

In this activity, it's very easy to lose the initial rhythm, so it's best for students who have already experienced feeling the pulse with their body.

In a circle, the teacher will give the initial pulse and the students will have to pass this pulse (it can be with clapping, tapping their feet, playing a percussion instrument, balls, bladders...) and it will always be passed in the same direction (clockwise). After they have done this activity a few times, you can vary it (by clapping your hands or tapping a drum twice), indicating that the direction in which the pulse should be passed should change. Remember to put the deaf students in a position where they can easily see you and realize that the direction will change.

Remember that when it comes to deaf students, the class should be conducted in LIBRAS and spoken, so that no student feels out of place. Also, make sure that these students don't have their own signs to communicate with each other (hearing and deaf), after all, not all students know Libras.

Another way that can be used when the teacher doesn't know LIBRAS is to use mime, always making the movements and the proposal very clear.

Music is not an external object, but belongs both outside and inside the body. The body expresses the music, but it also becomes the ear, transmuting itself into the music itself. The moment this happens, music and movement cease to be different and separate entities and, in their integration with man, become a unity. (FONTERRADA, 2008, p. 133)

Remember, music lessons will only make sense to deaf students if the classroom environment makes sense to them. In Daniel's case, the school environment he was in and where he had his music lessons made no sense to him at all. He hadn't been exposed to a form of language until then and his parents' attempt was for him to be able to hear, and he clearly rejected this possibility. After many moments of frustration at his parents' wishes, he was transferred to a bilingual school for the deaf.

9. DATA DESCRIPTION AND ANALYSIS

The methodological procedures were qualitative in nature, as already mentioned. The data was collected through interviews with deaf young people about how music plays a part in their lives and how they deal with music in everyday life.

Initially, the interviews were to take place in schools geared towards teaching deaf people, but due to the difficulty in accessing the schools found in the Greater Sao Paulo region, they were carried out in public places.

Some of the young people interviewed were approached at the Jabaquara and Santa Cruz subway stations in Sao Paulo. Other young people who were willing to be interviewed were contacted during the 12[a] International Fair of Technologies in Rehabilitation, Inclusion and Accessibility - REATECH - which took place in Sao Paulo in April 2013.

Browsing the *"niteriiet"* in search of bibliographic material for the research opened up the possibility of collecting data on the relationship between deaf young people and music on social networks and media. Blogs, Facebook and YouTube pages posted by young deaf people and musical groups made up of young deaf people completed the research data sources. Table 1 (one) below shows the interviews conducted and Table 2 (two) the networks and social media consulted.

Table 1 - interviews

Interviewees[9]	date	Interview location
DV - young female	27/03/2013	Santa Cruz metro station
BM - young female	21/04/2013	XII International Fair for Rehabilitation, Inclusion and Accessibility - REATECH
BP - young male	21/04/2013	XII International Trade Fair - REATECH
MS - young female	21/04/2013	XII International Trade Fair - REATECH

Table 2 - Social media consulted

social media	Projects	Location	City
Blog	The music of silence	Municipal school	Sao Paulo, SP

---

[9] To preserve the anonymity of the young people, they will only be referred to by the initials of their names.

Blog	The deaf: a path to music education	State Music Conservatory "Cora Pavan Capparelli",	Uberlândia, MG
Blog / FaceBook / YouTube	Ab'surdos Band	State Music Conservatory "Cora Pavan Capparelli",	Uberlândia, MG
Blog / FaceBook / YouTube	Surdodum	Ludovico Hearing and Language Educational Center Paroni (Ceal) - SE-SUBEP-DF public schools	Brasilia - DF
Blog / FaceBook / YouTube	Somda Skin	House of Drums	Recife -PB

9.1. INTERVIEWS WITH DEAF YOUNG PEOPLE

The young people contacted often refused to be approached for an interview, saying that music was of no interest to them as they were deaf. One young man with partial deafness, who didn't want to be identified, listened to music with a headset in only one ear. When this young man was asked if he liked music, he said no. Because he was deaf, music made no sense to him. But when asked what he was listening to, he said it was a pagode group that he liked.

In response to the questions asked during the interview, the following was obtained:

> Is music important in your life? Yes (why?) No (why?) Of the four interviewees, three answered yes and related music to feeling emotions. One young man replied that music made no sense to him.

> Describe how you perceive music?

All the interviewees described feeling the music through vibration and two of them, because they wore hearing aids, also felt it through their own hearing.

> When you listen to music, do you feel vibrations in specific parts of your body? Which parts? In general, the interviewees said they felt vibrations in their hands, feet and chest. Only one interviewee said she had never noticed it.

> Describe what it feels like in your body to listen to music.

In general, the sensation of feeling the music is pleasant. One of the young people said that the sensation could be one of happiness or fear, depending on the music.

> What kind of music do you like best?

The answers to this question were very varied: rock, funk, electronic music, country, pop, classical. One of the interviewees said she didn't like rock music because it gave her a bad feeling.

> Are you interested in vocal and instrumental music?

Three of the interviewees prefer instrumental music and only one said he preferred both instrumental and vocal music.

> Are you interested in learning music, a specific instrument?

The responses here were varied: one said she had no interest in learning to play a musical instrument, two young women expressed an interest in playing an instrument (one was a drummer and the other a pianist). The fourth girl had already studied the violin.

Below we can see the results of this survey in graph form, so that we can better analyze the data.

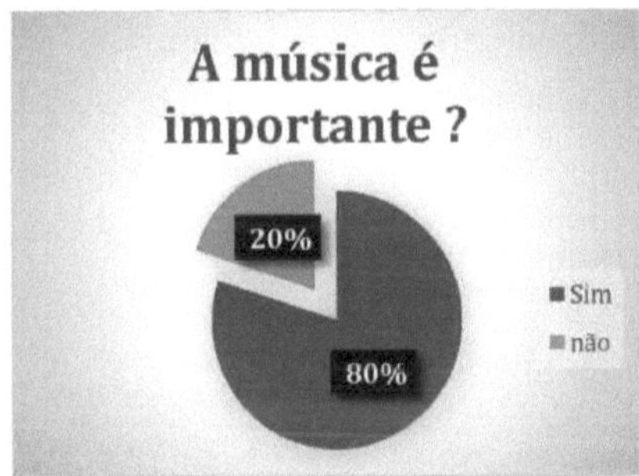

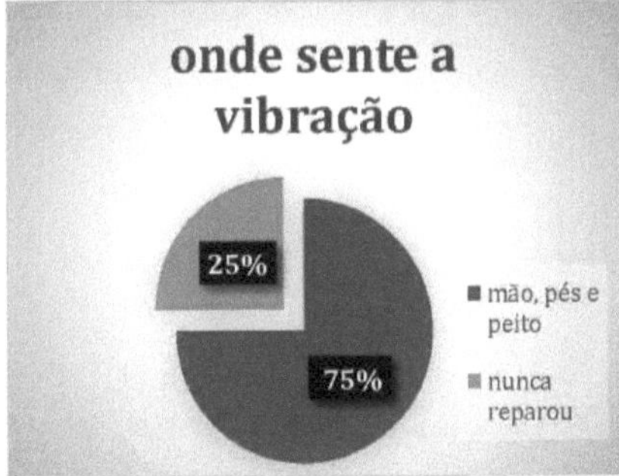

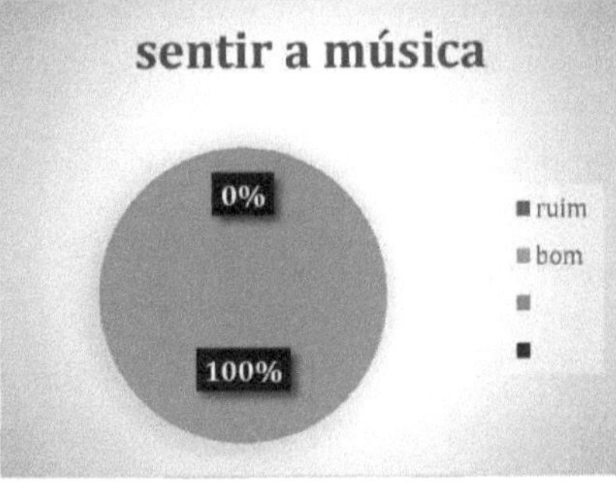

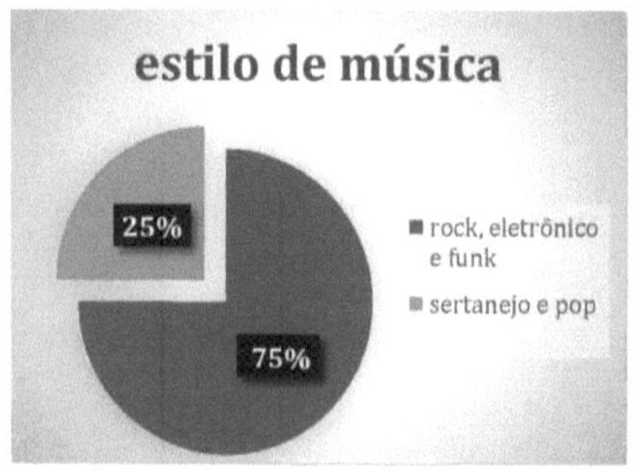

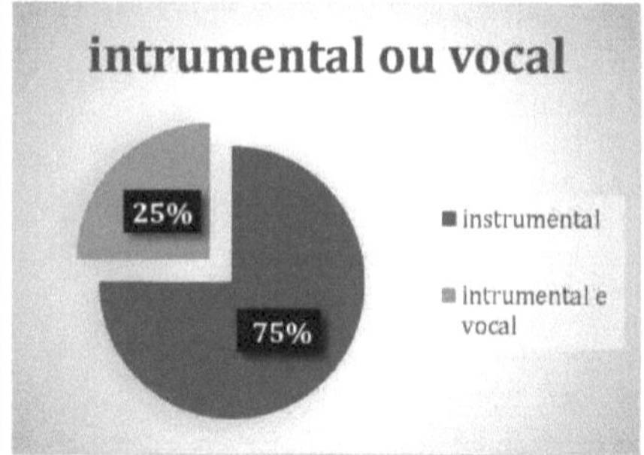

These ambiguities in the answers were found both in my interviews and in the interviews and reports found in the bibliography consulted. In her doctoral thesis, Regina Fink (2009) reports that during the classes she taught, the deaf children showed a complete interest in music. However, when she interviewed the students to find out what they remembered or what they had liked about the lessons, they said they didn't remember or didn't care much about what they had learned.

1.2. DEAF YOUNG PEOPLE IN MUSIC GROUPS

In Brazil, we can find some manifestations of musical groups in which deaf people play. Since, in cases of severe deafness, music is related to the perception of the vibrations of sound waves (and not properly to hearing), percussion instruments are preferred in the musical practice of deaf people.

The projects found during my search for blogs and websites are described below.

> **Music and silence project**

This project takes place in a municipal school in the city of Sao Paulo and began in 2005 in an unusual way. Fabio Novenuto, a conductor, needed a second school to continue his musical project, which had started in a school that only catered for listeners.

With the support of the principal of this second school, a school for deaf people, she confirmed the students' interest and started the Mùsica do Silêncio project in September 2012 with a group of 60 deaf students.

Below are some testimonies from young people taking part in the project.

<u>Elyver Cristina Conceiçao dos Santos</u> - student of the Mùsica do Silêncio project

"music is love"; "I received a piece of paper and my mother asked what it was. I said it was the band I liked. My mother was frightened, but my father let me take part, he's the one who brings me to the shows. "

<u>Henrique Gomes</u> - former student of the mùsica do silêncio project

" "Fàbio started teaching us the movements of music in the body and I started playing." "; " "I started to feel the noise and to play. I feel the vibration." "

<u>Fàbio Erico Alves Coelho</u> - student of the mùsica do silêncio project

" "Fàbio asks me to look and do the same. Fàbio teaches me and I do the same" "

<u>Kelvin Santos Magalhðes</u> - student of the mùsica do Silêncio project.

" "It's hard to play. But I learn with my friends. Which is good." "

<u>Fàbio Bovenuto</u> - conductor of the mùsica do silêncio project

"The deaf have their own musicality, right, and we've learned to respect that and take advantage of it. In fact, we have a very serious concern, which is not to impose our musicality on the deaf in our aesthetic sense."

> **Sound of the skin**

A group based in Recife, Pernambuco, made up of deaf people. The work is based on body perception and the study of the visual musical alphabet. To make it easier to visualize the pulse, they created a giant metronome that works with 4 light bulbs. These light up one at a time, according to the pulse of the music. The colors of the bulbs also help: green to muffle the sound and white to play loudly.

Member Iara says that she used to be sad and didn't like interacting with others, but after she joined the sound of the skin, the change began:

"I had the courage to take part, to beat the drums. I kept trying, persevering and I realized that deaf people can do it too. I'm deaf and have low vision, I can only see well out of one eye, but I feel capable. And I imagine: the deafblind person is also capable. He transforms this within himself and brings the dream into his life. It brings calm, it brings happiness... It's like a dream and through Som da Pele I've achieved that. It's improved my life a lot and brings me a lot of happiness," he says.

> **Surdodum**

This musical group began at the Ludovico Paroni Hearing and Language Educational Centre (Ceal) in Brasilia, a public school specializing in teaching the hearing-impaired. The work was based on rhythmic sensations, such as heartbeats, footbeats, handbeats, breathing, the clock, as well as visual information. Andréia, lead singer of the band Surdodum, who is profoundly deaf, said in an interview

"Hi, what's up? My name is Andréia [...] When I started singing, it was actually a bit difficult. At first I learned to sing Tim Maia's song "Azul da cor do mar". I kept trying and trying until I got it right. Then I got it, but it wasn't easy. It was hard, even though I don't listen, I listen with my eyes too." "

> **Deaf: The path to music publishing**

The project takes place in the city of Uberlândia - MG, at the Cora Pavan Capparelli State Music Conservatory. It was born after teacher Sarita Araùjo took on a deaf piano student, and consequently other deaf students followed. Sarita is also ~~deaf~~ and uses hearing aids. When she was young, watching a soap opera in which there was a white slave girl who played the piano, Sarita fell in love with the instrument and decided, despite her difficulties, to learn it. Years later, she graduated with a bachelor's degree in piano from the Federal University of Uberlândia.

The project began in 2002 and includes LIBRAS translators/interpreters to meet the communicative needs of the project. When a deaf student joins the project, they take part in two subjects: musicalization and instrument. In this context, with adapted curricula and didactic-pedagogical material, the musicalization classes are always linked to the instrument. Only after this preparation do the deaf students begin to attend the other subjects alongside the hearing students.

In 2011, the project launched its first sign manual for music: "Musical Terms in Brazilian Sign Language - LIBRAS".

This project led to the creation of the Ab'surdos Band, which released its CD and DVD in 2010.

1.3. YOUNG DEAF PEOPLE ON THE INTERNET

Continuing my research on the internet, I came across the blogs of two amazing people: Lak Lobato and Shoyi Chen.

Lakshmi, known as Lak Lobato, now 32, was born hearing, but lost her hearing at the age of 10. She was diagnosed with late sequelae of mumps, an irreversible diagnosis of bilateral profound deafness. She uses a cochlear implant, her mother tongue is Portuguese and she doesn't use LIBRAS as a second language.

In her text, she expresses the capacity for elasticity that a human brain can have. In the case of music, in her words: "For everything that moves, my brain imagines a sound. So the more rhythmic the movement, the closer it becomes to a melody. I love rhythmic movements because they become a real orchestra in my head. Sight is a great substitute for hearing".

Shaoyi Chen, president of the Chinese Deaf Association, lost his hearing at the age of fourteen. Before he fell ill and became deaf, Shaoyi studied music at school. After becoming deaf, he found it impossible to pursue his dream and so he gave up music. However, after 20 years of being deaf, he describes the experience of feeling silence and appreciating music:

"Since man is a thinking animal, even a person with physical disabilities can use his power of imagination and, if he has lost one of his senses, he can train and sharpen his other senses. Moreover, precisely because he has lost a kind of life that his heart yearns for, his experience of the world around him can usually be even more refined and even more genuine and closer to intuition. Therefore, he may probably have different feelings from those of a healthy person." "

As in Lak's text, he mentions the plasticity of the human brain. Brain plasticity, also known as neuroplasticity, is the brain's ability to readjust movements lost due to accidents, illnesses or congenital malformations, called bilateral amelia, which is the absence of limbs. For neuroplasticity to occur, you need motivation, psychic strength.

Brain plasticity is the name given to the adaptive capacities of the central nervous system - its ability to modify its own structural organization and functioning. It is the property of the nervous system that allows structural alterations to develop in response to experience and as an adaptation to changing conditions and repeated stimuli. (RELVAS, 2007, p.7) (LOURO, 2012, p.114)

10. conclusion

We can therefore consider that music can be used in an inclusive context for deaf students, as long as the environment makes sense to them. Often, when we come across disabled students, our hands are tied, we don't know where to start or what to do so that they don't feel excluded from lessons. With the information presented in this paper, I hope to be able to help teachers establish a starting point in relation to this issue.

The fundamental role of the teacher is to be a tool that transfers knowledge to their students in a clear, objective way that optimizes the resources available in the reality in which they are inserted. Due to the inherent abstractness of music as an art form, the teacher must look for ways to transfer this knowledge to the students without making them lose interest in the lesson.

When the teacher has a hearing-impaired student, he or she should check the degree of the disability, whether the student is oral or gestural, whether the student has a hearing aid or cochlear implant, and whether the student has any form of disability other than deafness. As can be seen in the course of this work, a deaf person can feel inferior or incapable in relation to hearing people, so it is also important to know if this student has psychotherapeutic support, as well as to encourage the student with deafness to discover that even with a disability, he or she is capable of overcoming obstacles. After all, who hasn't experienced some difficulty or insecurity in their life?

As educator Viviane Louro puts it:

"Music is important because it is important for all people at all times in their lives, regardless of their abilities or difficulties. (...) Everyone is capable of learning it. It's just a matter of respecting everyone's possibilities and adapting it for those who have marked difficulties" (2006, p. 29).

This research has shown that it is possible to achieve the inclusion of body movement in the music classroom, thus improving the inclusion of hearing-impaired students. It's up to the teacher to find the resources that suit them best, always bearing in mind their availability in their work environment.

As a final result of my research, I was able to observe that for deaf people music only has any meaning if it is experienced in a context, such as going to a club or a party. Otherwise, it has no meaning, unless the deaf person in question has a hearing impairment, wears a hearing aid or has a cochlear implant. In this case, music becomes a form of interaction just like for any other young person.

In general, profoundly deaf people prefer music with a strong pulse, such as rock, electronic music, rap and funk.

When it comes to learning music, deaf people prefer to use low-pitched instruments or percussion instruments, because they have more reverberation of sound. The way a deaf person can "hear" music is by feeling it through vibration, which for them is a pleasant sensation. Normally this vibration is felt by the limbs at the tips of the body (hands and feet) and in the chest.

Music, even for deaf people, brings comfort and feelings, even if this is felt through vibrations.

As we have seen, there are various musical manifestations throughout Brazil involving deaf young people. Unfortunately, we still lack more comprehensive research in this area, since the little that has been produced is related to strictly therapeutic and rehabilitative purposes. And research in the field of music education usually takes place according to their own experiences and curiosities.

In the course of the interviews, the analysis of the literature and the material on the Internet, it was noted that deaf young people often show an interest in music, but both in the interviews carried out in this work and those conducted by the educator Regina Finck, it was noted that when these young people were interviewed, their answers were very brief, showing an almost indifference to music.

In view of this, the teacher will help the deaf student to feel confident and enthusiastic about the possibility of developing their musical aptitude and skills to the best of their ability.

11. REFERENCES

ARROYO, Margarete. School, youth and music: tensions, possibilities and paradoxes. **Em Pauta:** Revista do Programa de Pós Graduaçao em Mùsica - UFRGS, Porto Alegre, v. 18, p. 5-39, 2007.

ARROYO, Margarete. Young people, music and investigative paths. Uberlândia. **ArtCultura**, v.12, n.20, p.21-35,2010.

BRAZIL. MEC. School, adolescence and youth. In: BRASIL. MEC. **National Curriculum Parameters. 5ª a 8ª série**. vol.1. Brasilia: MEC, 1998. p. 103 - 132.

BRAZIL. Decree No. 5.626, 2006. Available at:

http://www.planalto.gov.br/cci-vil 03/Ato2004-2006/2005/Decreto/D5626.htm

Accessed on: August 5, 2012.

BRAZIL. Law 11.769/2008. Available at

http://www.planalto.gov.br/cci- vil 03/Ato2007-2010/2008/lei/L 11769.htm Accessed on: March 12, 2013.

FINCK, Regina. **Teaching music to deaf students**: a perspective for inclusive pedagogical action. Thesis (Education) Postgraduate Program in Education, Federal University of Rio Grande do Sul, 2009.

FONTERRADA, Marisa Trench de Oliveira, 1939 - **Of wefts and threads: an essay on music and education** / Marisa Trench de Oliveira Fonterrada. -2.ed. - Sao Paulo: Editora UNESP; Rio de Janeiro: Funarte, 2008.

LOURO, Viviane S. **Educaçao Musical e Deficiência: PROPOSTA PEDAGÓGICA.**

Sao José dos Campos, SP: Ed. do Autor, 2006.

LOURO, Viviane S.; ALONSO, Luis g.; MOLINA, Sidney. **Fundamentals of musical learning for people with disabilities.** 1ª edition - Sao Paulo: Ed. Som, 2012.

GONÇALVES, Dorcelita B.; OLIVEIRA, Marcos R. **Musical Terms in Brazilian Sign Language - LIBRAS.** 1st edition - Minas Gerais: Ed. Pessalâcia Ltda, 2011.

HAGUIARA-CERVELLINI, Nadir G., THE **hearing-impaired child and his reactions to music.** 1st edition - Sao Paulo: Ed. Moraes Ltda, 1986.

HAGUIARA-CERVELLINI, Nadir G., **A musicalidade do surdo representaçâo e estigma.** 1st edition - Sao Paulo: Ed Plexus, 2003.

SACKS, Oliver. **Seeing voices: a journey into the world of the deaf**; translated by Laura Texeira Motta. Sao Paulo: Companhia das Letras, 2010.

STOKOE, Patricia. **Body expression in preschool** / Patricia Stokoe, Ruth Harf; [translated by Beatriz A. Cannabrava]. - Sao Paulo: Summus, 1987.

Zanchetta, Alessandra Maria. **EDUCAÇAO MUSICAL E SURDEZ: ponto de partida do ensino de mùsica para crianças surdas no contexto de inclusao** - TCC work UNESP - Sao Paulo 2010.

Sites consulted

The Music of Silence on RedeTv. Available at:

http://www.youtube.com/watch?fea- ture=player detailpage&v=hKm2uH4dmww Accessed on: May 24, 2013.

Fetal hearing. Available at

http://bebedofiituro.mus.br/audicao-do-feto/ Accessed on: 02/01/2015

Deaf drummers draw attention when they play in maracatu in Recife. Available at:

http://g1.globo.com/pernambuco/carnaval/2013/noticia/2013/02/batuqueiros-surdos-   chamam-atencao-ao-tocar-em-maracatu-no-recife.html Accessed on May 24, 2013.

Blog Banda Surdodum. Available at: http://surdodum.com/ Accessed on May 24, 2013.

Grupo Surdodum - inclusion through music. Available at:

< http://www.you- tube.com/watch?v=F 1QU tXNy6w > Accessed September 3, 2013.

Music in the Sao Paulo municipal network. Available at:

< http://www.you- tube.com/watch?feature=player detailpage&v=nHfl3Bv6TAA Accessed on:
May 24, 2013.

The fetus as a listening being. Available at:

http://www. cefac.br/library/te- sesZ9a11156fd396244a7685611978945461.pdf accessed on:
03/01/2015

The Meaning of Music. Available at:

http://www.workersforjesus.com/dfi/s-49por.htm accessed on May 25, 2013.

Deafness and Music - is this union possible? Available at:

http://www.vendovo- zes.com/2007/11/surdez-e-msica-this-union-possible.html accessed on May
25, 2013.

TV   Globo   shows   music   project   with   deaf   schoolchildren.   Available   at:
http://www.youtube.com/watch?feature=player detailpage&v=i1w8yXZ1Hjs Accessed on: May 24, 2013.

History of the deaf. Available at:

https://pt.wikipedia.org/wiki/Hist%C3%B3ria of the deaf Accessed on: September 17, 2017

Mabel Gardiner Hubbard. Available at:

https://en.wikipedia.org/wiki/Mabel Gardiner Hubbard Accessed: September 17, 2017

Deaf students in higher education: reflections on inclusion. Available at:

http://www.scielo.br/pdf/cp/v40n139/v40n139a08 Accessed on: September 17, 2017

Etiological factors of hearing loss in children and adolescents at an APADA reference center

in Salvador - BA. Available at:

http://www.scielo.br/pdf/%0D/rboto/v72n1/a06v72n1.pdf Accessed on: September 17, 2017

39

Discourses on deafness: Disabilities, Difference, Uniqueness and the Construction of Meaning. Available at:

http://www.scielo.br/pdf/ptp/v26n1/a02v26n1 Accessed on: September 17, 2017

12. ANNEXES

QUESTIONNAIRE

Name:

Age:

E-mail:

facebook:

Work:

1. Oralized: Yes ( ) No ( )

2. Do you use a hearing aid or cochlear implant? Yes ( ) No ( ) If yes, which?

3. Do you like music? yes ( ) No ( ) Don't relate ( )

3.1 How does it relate to music?

( ) Internet (youtube / translation into pounds)

( ) hears through the media . Which media:___________________________

( ) Sing

( ) plays a musical instrument

( ) participates in a band / musical group

INTERVIEW

1. Is music important in your life?

Yes Why? No Why?

2. Describe how you perceive music?

2.1 - When you listen to music, do you feel vibrations in specific parts of your body? Which parts?

2.2 - Describe how your body feels when you listen to music.

3. What kind of music do you like best?

4. Are you interested in vocal and instrumental music?

5. Are you interested in learning music, a specific instrument?

INFORMED CONSENT FORM

Rua: Dr Bento Teobaldo Ferraz, 271

01140-070 – Barra Funda

PABX: (11) 3393-8546

INSTITUTE OF ARTS

INFORMED CONSENT FORM

We would like to ask for your permission to take part in a research project linked to a degree course in Music Education at UNESP's Arts Institute. The research will be carried out by student Thais da Silva Natal, under the supervision of Prof. Dr. Margarete Arroyo.

This research project focuses on deaf young people and their relationship with music. Interviews will be conducted and a questionnaire administered to deaf young people who are interested in taking part in the research; audio recordings will be made for later analysis, if the interviewees allow it. These recordings will only be used for scientific and academic purposes.

______________________________ ____________________

Prof. Dr. Margarete Arroyo Thaís da Silva Natal

RG 10.142.764-SSP-MG RG 42.139.448-1 SSP-SP

I,   , have been informed of the objectives

specified above, in a clear and detailed manner. I have received specific information about the procedure in which I will be involved. All my questions have been answered clearly, and I know that I can ask for further clarification at any time by calling (11) 96760-6540.

I am free to withdraw my consent to take part in the research. I declare that I have received a copy of this informed consent form.

Young person's name: ________________ Signature ____________________

Responsible Signature

Date __/__/____

Signature of the person responsible for the research:

____

Thais da Silva Natal

Printed by Books on Demand GmbH, Norderstedt / Germany